WHAT IS WISDOM?

WHAT is WISDOM?

A Collection of Practical Thoughts for Better Decisions in Life

KAYVAN KIAN

TO THE MOON PUBLISHING

New York, New York

WHAT IS WISDOM?
A Collection of Practical Thoughts for Better Decisions in Life

ISBN   978-1-5445-2438-2   *Hardcover*
       978-1-5445-2436-8   *Paperback*
       978-1-5445-2437-5   *Ebook*

Library of Congress Control Number: 2021916853

The material in this book is adapted from
articles written by Kayvan Kian that originally
appeared on *Forbes.com* and *McKinsey.com*.

TO THE MOON PUBLISHING
New York, New York

Author Photograph by Giovanni Siani
Graphic Design by Afitha de Rijk–Voeten and Tina Rataj
Illustrations by Teresa Muniz

Fortuna Eruditis Favet

—Latin Phrase

Dedicated to the Once and Future You.

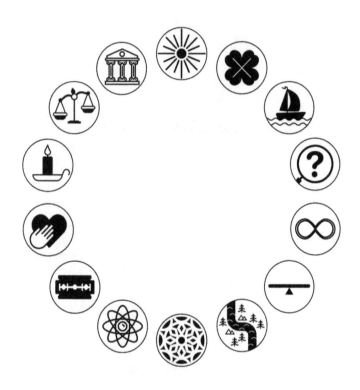

Contents

Welcome

Would you consider yourself *wise* when it comes to the choices you make? Most likely, at least *wiser* than last year or last decade. Wisdom can come with the years, through experience, study, and practice. Whether you want it or not, your upcoming decisions will lead to positive or negative consequences, foreseen or unforeseen, intended or unintended, big or small. You are not, however, the first person confronted with difficult life decisions.

This book will share the hard-fought experience, lessons, and thoughts of philosophers who did their best before you over the past millennia.

The sociologist William Bruce Cameron once wrote, "*Not everything that can be counted counts. Not everything that counts can be counted.*" In today's world, we often attempt to resolve tough questions by reducing a problem or opportunity to something that can be counted in order to weigh the costs and benefits, regardless of the risks, scale, or nature of the decision. This approach, if taken mindlessly, can disconnect us from the complexities of the real world. It can miss the most important "noncountable" criteria for the decision at hand, lead us to an unfounded sense of confidence, and therefore cause more problems than it tries to solve.

In an uncertain world with much at stake, broadening your perspective *beyond* what can be counted can increase the chances of better decisions. In the coming chapters, you will get the opportunity to playfully practice unique *ways of thinking* and approaches to problems, each introduced by another philosopher from the past.

Thales can help you spot patterns you might otherwise be missing. Cleobulus cautions against getting too comfortable during prosperous times or too uncomfortable when times are tough. Nietzsche can help you live with fewer regrets, while Occam can save you time and energy when making decisions. These and many others you'll meet in the coming pages, with room to write your own thoughts, ideas, and more.

The goal of this book *isn't* to promote a certain way of thinking above the other. Each situation is unique, and certain approaches will be more appropriate in certain cases. In essence, the main goal here is to practice *switching between* these ways of thinking. Just as the ability to *switch between* gears in a vehicle provides more safety and freedom, the ability to switch between these ways of thinking will also bring you numerous benefits.

It will help you better adapt to a changing environment and prevent you from making unnecessary and irreversible mistakes. It can help you make a better distinction between what matters and what doesn't and how to make regret-free decisions. It can give you the courage to take action when the opportunity arises, the prudence to pause when perspective is needed, and the diligence to follow through to get closer to where you want to be. In other words, this ability to *switch* can help you answer the question, *What Is Wisdom?*

Along the way, you could even develop your own life philosophy, which you can pass on to future generations as your legacy. Regardless of the final result, may you enjoy with each step the sense of mastery, freedom, and wonder that awaits you.

Cleobulus Can Help You Survive Both Prosperous and Hard Times

f you've been pursuing your dreams for a while, you know that life is filled with both highs and lows: times that are prosperous and times that are tough. On both sides of the coin, it can be tempting to respond in an excessive way. When times are good, we may be tempted to take it easy and stop doing the things that led to our success.

In bad times, when things look hopeless, we may be tempted to despair or give up entirely. Both reactions are understandable but carry significant risk.

To best deal with the good and bad times that will inevitably come our way, we can look to the wisdom of Cleobulus, who was a Greek poet in the sixth and seventh centuries. He was also counted as one of the Sages of Greece, or Seven Wise Men.

Like many of the pre-Socratic philosophers, much of Cleobulus's work is lost to us. However, this quote has survived and endures to this day: "Do not be arrogant in prosperity. If you fall into poverty, do not humble yourself; know how to bear the changes of fortune with nobility."

To see how we can apply the lessons of this quote in practice, let's look at contrasting scenarios you may face.

Being Swept Away by Circumstances

There are times when, for instance, a company catches lightning in a bottle: demand goes through the roof, bringing in mountains of new revenue and causing unprecedented levels of growth. To use a phrase from the startup world, it's the "hockey stick" model of growth. After tinkering and skating by for several years, a young company hits an inflection point and sees surging growth.

Conversely, many companies fail to hit this point after many years of effort. Promises haven't been fulfilled. Perhaps there's a problem with production that's delayed the product and evaporated customer interest, or the orders haven't been coming in despite customers saying they were excited. Whatever the case, there's no hockey stick. Growth is flat.

As different as these situations seem, leaders on both sides may feel an urge to be carried away by external circumstances, and their actions may reflect it.

Instead of figuring out what it is that's working so well and building further on that, leaders of the successful company might indulge by spending extravagantly, making reckless moves, or treating people with a certain disregard. In their mind, the good times won't stop rolling, so what does it matter how much they spend or how they act?

Meanwhile, instead of learning from their mistakes, trying something new, or finding a way to minimize current losses, the ones leading the struggling company might let go or give up. They might assume their misfortunes are permanent, lose their inner strength, will, and courage, and adopt the self-fulfilling mantra: *Who cares if I take any action? It won't matter anyway.*

Living without Illusions

When we get carried away by external circumstances, we can make dangerous mistakes. One such mistake is assuming our actions carry no significant consequences. This of course is not true. Even without the consideration of external results, our actions shape who we are and who we become, in both prosperous and hard times. Our external circumstances don't define us, but how we *respond* to those circumstances—which is *within* our control—does define our character.

Another mistake is underestimating the role of luck, especially when we're experiencing success. When everything you do turns to gold, you may lose touch with the complexities of reality. It might be tempting to claim these results as the fruit of your own genius and hard work and consider them confirmation of your otherworldly talents. Astronomical profits or a successful project can make it inconceivable that things might turn out differently next year, let alone tomorrow.

As Cleobulus shows us, there is no guarantee that things will continue the same as they are today, which should offer hope to the hopeless and a word of caution to those who rest on their laurels.

This word of caution, of course, isn't meant to create worry or anxiety. It is meant to prevent unnecessary and irreversible mistakes. It is meant to make sure you're not surprised when you're sent back to the drawing board of life. It is meant to encourage you to cultivate things that no one can ever take away from you: your will, creativity, unique strengths, clarity of thought, and more. As the philosopher-king Marcus Aurelius said, "Never let the future disturb you. You will meet it, if you have to, with the same weapons of reason which today arm you against the present."

Looking Back from the Future

Look at your life today. Not yesterday, not tomorrow, but today. Which parts are going well? Which parts are not? How are things at work? How are your relationships with family and friends? How are your childhood dreams? Which things are going well that you might be taking for granted? Which things might you be giving up on? Which area of your life would be helped most by Cleobulus's thinking?

What would you tell yourself if you were to come back to this day decades from now? Are you meeting with that potential investor or canceling because you don't think it will matter? Are you setting aside something for the future or spending it all as if you'll never run out?

Cleobulus teaches us not to trust both good and bad times. He shows us that if we trust *ourselves* instead, we may "bear the changes of fortune with nobility."

Thoughts, Ideas & More...

Thoughts, Ideas & More...

Heraclitus Can Help You Feel Empowered in a Changing World

We live in a world that can be described as VUCA: volatile, uncertain, complex, and ambiguous. Things are changing so fast that it's hard to know what's coming next, and since the world is more interconnected than ever before, many would say they aren't even sure what they *need* to know. That said, you could argue that things have always been this way.

Two millennia ago, the Greek philosopher Heraclitus remarked that "the only constant is change." However, it's fair to say some periods in history have felt more VUCA than others. If you feel that your environment is changing at a faster pace and that you need to continuously expect the unexpected in an unpredictable, unclear world, you most certainly are not alone.

Such an environment can pose a tremendous struggle for many. When change is happening all around you, it can create a sense of overwhelm and give rise to a temptation to cling to how things used to be. Entrepreneurs, for example, might miss "the good old days" before their organization experienced rapid growth, back when making decisions was easier and they knew everyone's first names.

Whether you're lost in a sense of nostalgia or simply overwhelmed, you may be reluctant to engage with the *here and now*.

What Is Happening in Your World?

Here's a short exercise to better understand your own context. Think about everything that has happened over the past six to twelve months, and list the events that had a significant effect on you. The points you note can be positive or negative, local or global, and so forth.

The following guiding questions may help:

Globally

- Which news headlines struck you in the last six to twelve months?
- What political and economic events are present in your mind?

Locally

- What happened in your region, city, and/or neighborhood?
- What have you grown accustomed to that was not part of your life a year ago?

Personally

- What happened in your personal life and the lives of those around you?
- How is your life different today in comparison to a year ago?

Take some time and reflect on the lists above. What feelings arise when you think about these events and situations? How do you think the people around you feel about these changes?

What Is *Within* Your Control?

As you can see, even in the past six to twelve months, your world has likely been in a constant state of change. Heraclitus has another quote that can help us stay aware of this undeniable fact:

> *"You could not step twice into the same rivers; for other waters are ever flowing onto you."*

In a VUCA world where change is the only constant, the mindset that can help you thrive comes from the ancient Stoics: *a radical focus on what you can control*. At any given moment, there is an infinite number of things *outside* of your control, while at the same time, there are also things *within* your control. How good are you at making a distinction between the two?

What would it mean to have *a radical focus on what you can control* today? What would you do differently in life? With this focus, where would you invest your time, heart, and energy?

This mindset is of course not an excuse for apathy, nor is it about encouraging you to walk around without caring what happens outside of your control or shrugging off the ups and downs in your life. The aim of this lens is to empower you to achieve the opposite of apathy and help you cultivate an active attitude in life.

You *can't* control the wind, but you *can* adjust your sail. You *can't* control how many new clients you sign, but you *can* control whom you reach out to, which improvements you make, the energy you bring, and the effort you put into your follow-up. You *can't* control whether you'll get your desired budget, but you *can* control how you repurpose all the personal, relational, organizational, societal, and perhaps even metaphysical resources you *already* have access to.

"Doing what you can with what you've got" means caring about your life so much that by focusing on what you *can* control, you *can* invest all your thoughts, efforts, and energy in ways that can make a difference.

Thoughts, Ideas & More...

Thoughts, Ideas & More...

Thoughts, Ideas & More...

Socrates Can Help You Prevent Irreversible Mistakes

Success has a way of breeding overconfidence in one's decision making, especially after it follows a longer period of good results. It's tempting to bask in the glory of a job well done and assume that things will continue to go well because of your sound judgment.

In these scenarios, you also run the risk of surrounding yourself with "yes people" who encourage, applaud, and approve of everything you do. Trouble comes when a decision must be made for the future of the organization—say a new product launch, geographic expansion, or merger—and the overconfident leader "just knows what to do." What worked in the past might not work now. The situation might require fresh perspectives to find the right solution or risk charting a course that leads to an irrecoverable mistake.

This scenario illustrates the value of *skepticism*, exemplified by the Greek philosopher Socrates, who was known as the "gadfly of Athens" for the way he always asked critical questions. His famous quote "I know that I know nothing" demonstrates Socrates's skeptical attitude.

The mantra for skeptics could be summed up as *Is that really so?* This line of thinking is not meant to halt all forms of decision making or cause paralysis by analysis but rather to ensure that decisions are well thought out.

A skeptical lens is useful for preventing bad, possibly irrecoverable decisions (such as those that lead to bankruptcy) and can help seize opportunities that we might otherwise overlook. And yet, skepticism could become an underused tool because people often prefer the feeling they get when their ideas are confirmed rather than criticized.

Think for a moment about yourself: when assembling teams, much can depend on who you ask to be your team members. Do you intentionally select only those who are "on your side," or do you ask critics to join as well?

After completing an important document such as a business idea or essay, you might feel relieved that the job is finally done, especially if the writing process was difficult. How many rounds of feedback and iterations would you like to have after you've "finished" and from whom?

At the end of a conversation, you might be very good at articulating the reasons to make a certain decision; however, how well can you describe other (opposing) points of view? And how could these other perspectives inform and improve the quality of your decision?

Building "Skeptic Capital" before You Need It

Certain opportunities may come along only once in a lifetime, some initiatives require decades before the fruits of your investments appear, and seemingly minor missteps can close important doors forever. Therefore, you often won't have the chance to learn from experience, delay a decision, get better information about the future, or afford plain bad luck.

In these situations, you can use your "skeptic capital." Who are the family members, friends, and colleagues who feel comfortable helping you hit the brakes, think deeper, and change the course before it's too late? Have you ever considered developing the size and quality of this skeptic capital over time?

You may already have these people in your life without noticing how helpful they could be. Just think of the people you might avoid because you find their constant questions annoying. Those could be the exact right people to include in your circle of skeptics.

You may also find valuable skeptics a bit further from home or work. Maybe you respect particular entrepreneurs for their beneficial experience and business acumen. You could invite them into a role where they challenge your ideas to ensure you see them from all angles.

In meetings, for instance, you may appoint someone to ask *"Is that really so?"* in as many ways as possible. You can also, as a team, envision your most skeptical customer and address the questions and objections they would likely have about your new product or service.

Of course, if you don't have anyone around to help right now, you can always infuse a healthy dose of doubt in your life yourself. For example, if something goes well, you might assume that the underlying decision making was brilliant and wise. But what if you were just lucky? What would this mean for the next time you're in a similar situation?

Creating (Ir)reversible Momentum

Again, the goal of skepticism isn't to halt momentum. It's meant to help you become better aware of risky blind spots and find smart ways to deal with them.

For instance, if you're about to make an irreversible decision, could you first design a small-scale pilot, build in a trial period, or arrange a money-back guarantee? What if you crowdfunded the investment funds you needed rather than all of it coming out of pocket?

Or if you're about to make a decision that is too reversible, could you build in significant penalties or fees for any party attempting to reverse the decision? What would "burning the bridges behind you" look like in this scenario?

Over time, your skepticism can grow further and become a more natural part of your daily life to prevent irreversible mistakes. And who knows? Right now, you might already be hearing the voice of Socrates wondering *is that really so?*

Thoughts, Ideas & More...

Thoughts, Ideas & More...

Nietzsche Can Help You Live a Regret-Free Life

Whether you're fresh out of school or settled in your career, you can find yourself so busy in your daily responsibilities that you set aside—or lose sight of—the bigger picture of your life and career. You might be feeling that way right now.

Perhaps there's a new hobby you'd like to explore, a company you want to start, or a big life change you're interested in making. But for whatever reason, you keep pushing the decision weeks or months down the road, or you don't have the opportunity to deeply consider it.

On the other hand, you might not be struggling with busyness as much as you are with boredom. If you've ever gone to work and found yourself restless about how familiar it all feels, you might be suffering from "bore-out."

Whether you're too bogged down because of your daily responsibilities, or you're bored to tears at your desk, the nineteenth-century German philosopher Friedrich Nietzsche might be able to offer you some perspective.

Nietzsche popularized a thought experiment that stretches back to classical antiquity called "eternal recurrence." It is the idea that the universe—all of existence and every bit of energy—has been recurring and will continue to recur an infinite number of times. Think of it this way: however you choose to spend your time today, that's exactly how your day will occur an infinite number of times in the future.

This is not meant to be applied as a worldview but rather a thought experiment that asks, *how would you feel* if you were to repeat this part of your life again and again, exactly the same way, an infinite number of times?

Giving Our Daily Choices Added Weight

Some might answer, "Thanks for asking. I like the life I've built and what I'm working toward. If I had the choice, I would do it all over again." If that's where you fall, that's wonderful. This thought experiment is still useful in bringing awareness to your current state of mind.

But what if your answer doesn't elicit a smile on your face and a twinkle in your eye? If the choices you make don't create experiences you'd be thrilled to repeat an infinite number of times, then *what would it take* to get one step closer to the life you want?

Without making drastic changes to your day-to-day life, you could start by *thinking differently* about *existing* situations without changing them. For instance, you can choose to *discover* new meaning in your *existing* work by noticing what you're *already* contributing in all its richness—from creating something of significance to preventing something undesirable.

Inspiring Us to the Moon and Beyond

Thinking differently about what you're *already* doing might make your work only slightly more bearable. Nietzsche's thought experiment might therefore illuminate the fact that bigger changes are needed. If what you're doing doesn't meet the bar for eternal recurrence—and you don't believe it will, even by changing your perspective—then what bigger decisions might you need to make?

By putting infinite weight on your decisions, eternal recurrence asks you about the nature of your activities: *why* do you do them? Because things just *turned out* in a certain way or because you *want* to do them? When you regularly go back to the drawing board, you may find that you're living a more self-chosen path that is built to withstand the challenge of repetition.

Eternal recurrence helps you focus sharply on what is important to *you* and make the choice *you* believe is best, every moment of every day of every month of every year. This thought experiment is therefore also an antidote for regret. Not because things will turn out exactly the way you would want them to (they rarely do), but when today echoes on into eternity, you will always have the peace of mind that you did the right thing given the infinite number of choices you had at each moment.

Thoughts, Ideas & More...

Thoughts, Ideas & More...

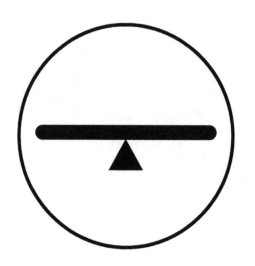

Aristotle Can Help You Find Meaning in Building Your Own Character

"We become just by performing just actions, temperate by performing temperate actions, brave by performing brave actions."

—Aristotle

An entrepreneur felt like giving up on a Tuesday afternoon: the new version of a product turned out to have some unexpected flaws, one of the co-founders wasn't reachable abroad, and a potential investor had postponed the decision to invest by another week.

In a world that feels more volatile, uncertain, complex, and ambiguous, where the results of one's actions are not always as hoped for, it isn't always apparent how to discover meaning in one's work. And therefore, it can feel difficult to find, in the words of Nietzsche, a *why* that can help you bear any *how*. In the view of the ancient Greek philosopher Aristotle, an often-overlooked realm where one can *always* find meaning in these situations is *virtues*: character traits that are considered to be positive.

Think of people you respect and who inspire you. Most likely, you feel this way not only because of *what* they have accomplished in life but also because of *who* they have become in the process. In other words, because of their character.

What character traits, or virtues, would you like to embody over time? And how are you making use of everyday opportunities to practice these? When times are difficult, building virtues could be the single source of meaning to help you pull through, as they have done for countless others in the past. Many philosophies and schools of thought even considered building good character to be the main goal of human life.

Courage, kindness, humility, diligence, honesty, patience, generosity, tolerance, compassion—the good news is that you don't need to block extra time to exercise these virtues in your busy day. Virtues are trained not *on top* of your daily life but *as part of* it, and the more challenging the day is, the bigger the training opportunity. The main question, however, is how consciously are you practicing these traits for their own sake, and how are you making the most of each unique opportunity?

When a potential investor postpones the decision to invest, which virtue might the entrepreneur be training? Perhaps patience. For when is the *only* time one can practice patience? When one really, really doesn't want to, of course. In the same way, the *only* time to practice courage is in the presence of real fear.

As easy as this might sound, it takes hard work and much practical experience to find the "golden mean" in a particular situation: which virtue is necessary? Which level is sufficient? For instance, when it comes to giving a birthday gift, how well can you tell the difference among stinginess, *generosity*, and wastefulness? When it comes to a conversation during lunch, the difference between boorishness, *wit*, and buffoonery? And when it comes to someone you know well, the difference among flakiness, *friendship*, and intrusiveness? As Aristotle said about finding and practicing these "golden means" in each context, it is about the right amount, at the right time, tailored to the situation at hand.

Think about an important action you took in the past year with the intention of helping someone, and answer the following questions for yourself:

- What is the context in which this commendable action took place?

- How would you consider this action significant?

- What would (less heroic) others most likely have done in the same situation?

- What are the values and positive character traits you exemplified?

- What are the positive consequences of this action for the other, you, and your broader community?

- What could others learn from this action?

- How have you prevented irreversible mistakes or harm?

- Have you made similar decisions in the past, indicating a unique pattern?

- How proportional was the practice of virtue to the situation at hand?

- Could you have done more? Should you have done less?

- Is there anything you would have done differently?

Looking forward, which virtues would you want to further develop to build your own character? And what are the best situations to practice them in? Are there any activities in the coming days that you won't particularly enjoy? Which virtues could you develop through these unique opportunities?

Thoughts, Ideas & More...

Thoughts, Ideas & More...

Thoughts, Ideas & More...

Bruce Lee Can Help You Adapt and Overcome Obstacles

Have you ever experienced a time in your life where it seemed like everything was going wrong, just as you were trying to pursue a dream or start a new initiative?

Your budget request was denied for a second time.

The first tasting of your new recipes didn't turn out as expected.

The partnership you envisioned didn't come to fruition.

The feedback on your draft wedding speech was disappointing.

In moments like these, when setbacks seem to stack on top of each other, it can feel as if the world is actively working against you. It's easy to get discouraged and tempting to just give up.

But given what's at stake for yourself, your teams, your organization, or even society, you might decide to roll up your sleeves and find a new way of doing things. This requires new levels of flexibility, adaptability, and resourcefulness. As martial arts legend Bruce Lee said, you will need to *"be water."*

This philosophy—born of Taoism and popularized by Lee—is about finding a different way forward when your path is blocked, just like water does when a river gets jammed.

Let's take a look at the characteristics of water and how they could apply to your life.

Water Adapts and Finds a Way

The notion "be water" came from an interview in which Lee said, "*Now you put water in a cup; it becomes the cup. You put water into a bottle; it becomes the bottle. You put it in a teapot, and it becomes the teapot. Now water can flow, or it can crash. Be water, my friend.*"

His point was this: Water is fluid. It's formless. Whatever situation you put water in, it adapts. Nobody would use terms like *rigid*, *unchanging*, *unyielding*, or *inflexible* to describe water.

When water in a river hits a rock, what does it do? Does it stop and complain, "Why did life bring this rock into my path?" No, it simply slides around the rock and moves along. It doesn't underreact, overreact, or stop. It flows, to the best of its ability, exactly as it needs, depending on the situation.

In a world that is VUCA—volatile, uncertain, complex, and ambiguous—you can benefit from studying the way water adapts and overcomes anything in its way.

In your life, is there a challenge that gives you an opportunity to "be water" or a situation where you can *go with the flow*?

Water Never Gives Up

The baseball player Babe Ruth once said, "*It's hard to beat someone who never gives up.*"

Water never gives up. It's relentless and flexible on its way to its destination. If it can, a river will flow in a straight line. If necessary, it will adapt its direction around obstacles to still move forward and reach where it wants to go, not always taking the *shortest* but the *fastest* path.

When that budget request fails, what would be an unconventional way to still get your initiative started?

First tastings of new recipes rarely turn out perfect. What's the smallest change that could make the biggest difference?

When one door closes, many others might open. Is there another partnership you can pursue?

Instead of a wedding speech, can you write a creative wedding song that will touch the couple's hearts?

Most people don't want challenges, setbacks, or difficult situations to come their way. But it happens anyway. And when it does, you have a chance to adapt and overcome.

"Be Water" at Work

That's not to say you should "be *only* water." In many organizations, people write tried-and-tested protocols with specific steps that must be taken and make detailed project plans to reach a goal. But is it really possible to foresee and prepare for each future event?

Plans can be helpful. Protocols can work. Practical support from your colleagues for your idea can make things easier. But there's a risk that these things can unknowingly become a goal in themselves and therefore a distraction. As always, it's important not to mix up *means* and *ends* and to have a *clear distinction* between the two. What's your *real* goal, and how can you "be water" at the right moments to get there as smoothly as possible?

Often, unforeseen setbacks arise in frustrating ways. The obvious reflex could be to complain, blame, give up, or use "unstoppable force" in an attempt to move an immovable obstacle. But life is too complex to be tamed in all its dimensions. The lesson here is this: *dare to improvise*. Enjoy being free, versatile, and flexible. You might come up with elegant, novel, and tailor-made solutions for unexpected problems—just as water beautifully improvises on its way down the mountain.

Take a moment to think of one thing that is currently in your way and how to go *around* this obstacle to reach your goals instead of *against* it. Or better yet, don't *think* and just *"be* water."

Thoughts, Ideas & More...

Thoughts, Ideas & More...

Thales Can Help
You Recognize
Patterns on Time

These days, many find themselves in the middle of a constant stream of ever-increasing information from more and more sources: email, news outlets, social media, messaging apps, along with conversations with colleagues, friends, and family.

Given the amount, complexity, and often inconsistency of all this information, it can be difficult to make important decisions—or even trivial ones. How confident are you that you're making the right distinctions at the right moment, especially when they matter most? How easily can you tell the difference between a real signal and plain noise, between an important message and an unconventional messenger, between a root cause and a superficial symptom?

What can at times prove helpful in this regard is not necessarily trying to process each piece of information further in *isolation* but being able to spot *patterns*. Taking a step back to examine the larger picture over time can help you improve your judgment in everyday decision making. However, this can be especially challenging if you're just beginning your career.

Those who've been through much in the past—recessions, bankruptcies, wars, and their buildup—can be better equipped to notice a pattern on time and say, "I've seen this before." They know life's ups and downs and can navigate good and bad times with the appropriate measures because they've learned from experience.

For those who are less experienced, this can be more of a challenge. They may understand the idea of noticing patterns intellectually but, in practice, find it hard to apply this perspective. In turn, they might struggle to know what they should act on and what they can safely ignore.

If you'd like to become better at spotting patterns before it's too late, the wisdom of the ancient philosopher Thales (considered by many to be the first philosopher in the Western tradition) could help you, regardless of how much life experience you have.

Patterns in Olives, Water, and Stars

Not much is known about Thales, but it was said that one time, while he was gazing up at the stars,

Thales fell into a well. This story is often shared as an example of how philosophers, in their reflection on reality, can lose touch with everyday life.

However, what is often omitted is *why* he would typically look up at the sky: Thales was a good observer of the weather and, in many ways, much more practical than you might think. Expanding his knowledge of meteorological processes helped him predict many events, apparently including the solar eclipse of May 28, 585 BC.

During another year, he also predicted a surplus of olives. Before others found this out, Thales had already rented himself all of the olive presses in Miletus.

Out of touch? Hardly. When you get to know Thales better, you can understand why Aristotle said of him, "In this way, he proved that philosophers can easily be wealthy."

Thales's search for improving his understanding of the world and its patterns wasn't limited to any scale. He was interested in astronomy as well as the nature of matter (he was known for his position that "*all is water*"). Furthermore, he practiced geometry, mathematics, and engineering but most of all, avoided superstitions. He tried to explain natural phenomena without looking for a supernatural cause.

Which Patterns Do You Want to Discover?

If you want to improve your ability to notice patterns in life in order to make better decisions, there are many things you could do, starting today.

First, you might consider journaling to better understand your *own* patterns. Take notes on the thoughts you have and the actions you take in certain circumstances. In the moment, patterns can be hard to spot. As you look back over your notes, however, you may begin to see patterns related to many aspects of your life. Is there a recurring theme when it comes to how you feel during the day? What do you notice about your personal and professional relationships? How about the way you deal with difficult circumstances?

Second, you can improve this skill by learning from the experiences of others. Read (auto)biographies, watch documentaries, and take an interest in other people's life stories. Which patterns have others noticed in their lives, and is there anything you can relate to? Are there any predictions you could make about yourself based on these? Would you want to strengthen, weaken, or even break any of these personal patterns?

Finally, on a more abstract level, you could consider that everything that happens around you today is part of a larger pattern that you may notice and study on different scales: astronomy, physics, biology, chemistry, history, sociology, economics, ethics, and more. Which fields and their patterns would you like to learn more about? What is the best way to do that given the time, energy, means, and access that you currently have? Are there any fields you would like to contribute to?

All in all, it could be worthwhile to invest a little every day to search for commonalities and dissimilarities between your observations over time. Instead of exposing yourself solely to isolated information about today, you could improve your understanding of short- and long-term patterns that have occurred since the times of Thales. Enjoy the discoveries that are waiting for you. Just make sure you don't get so fascinated that you forget about a special ancient pattern involving stars and wells.

Thoughts, Ideas & More...

Thoughts, Ideas & More...

Democritus Can Help You Connect Theory with Practice

"*The most dangerous thing about an academic education is that it enables my tendency to over-intellectualize stuff, to get lost in abstract thinking instead of simply paying attention to what's going on in front of me.*"
—David Foster Wallace

The ancient thinker Democritus is considered by many to be the father of modern science and is known for his theory that everything is made of atoms.

He believed that knowledge was something to be reached through the intellect, based on observations through the senses. In other words, theory couldn't be detached from everyday experience.

This line of thinking isn't just appropriate for science classrooms and laboratories. It's applicable in daily life, too. When you pay closer attention to what is happening right in front of you, you will notice important signals you would've otherwise missed.

Intellectual people, especially those fresh from university, are often eager to grasp new concepts and ways of thinking. However, this can lead to a trap of overlooking what is actually happening.

To be sure you don't become lost or disconnected, the advice is therefore to *"look and act closer."* When you do this, life becomes richer. You taste the food you're eating and hear the music that's playing. You're able to understand the conversation instead of just being physically present. You receive immediate feedback from your environment and can adapt to it instead of thinking, "Well, the book said this," or "That's not what I thought would happen." Democritus's thinking can bring our observations and actions closer to the world as it is.

What Would Democritus Do?

As you can see, this "inductive method" pushes you to get in touch with how things *actually* work, not just how they *should* work. It's rooted in this idea of being connected to your environment and reacting to the feedback you receive. Think of Thomas Edison as he worked on the light bulb. His focus was on the results of each experiment; he continuously refined and tested his formulas and scientific principles.

His work exemplified this quote, which is attributed to many but actually has unknown origins: "*In theory, there is no difference between practice and theory. In practice, there is.*"

Books and other trusted and curated sources of information are a great way to gather knowledge, but they are simply a jumping-off point for the acquisition of wisdom, which also comes from practice and experience, as well as opening your eyes to that experience.

Thankfully, cultivating a mindset that is in touch with the "world of atoms" is easier than you might think. It starts with using your senses more often. When you're out on a walk, for example, don't just see the path in front of you. *Listen* to the world. *Smell* the air. *Touch* the rocks and plants.

This practiced form of observation will also serve you well at work. When you finish a meeting with a client or employee, ask yourself, *What did I see or hear firsthand during that interaction?* Were these observations relevant? Did they reduce uncertainty? In other words, were they *informational*? These reflective questions ensure you don't overlook or forget the signals your environment was giving you.

Don't be afraid to experiment or break out of your routine. Let's say instead of writing a message, you call a friend. Did that work better to de-escalate the situation? What can you learn from your new observations?

Finally, cultivate a curiosity around how things *actually* work. Expose yourself to different areas of society to see how others do their jobs. Do they match your notions of how that work was done? You might be surprised—and enlightened—by what you find, not only in *theory* but also in *practice*.

Thoughts, Ideas & More...

Thoughts, Ideas & More...

Occam Can Help You Save Time and Energy

"When you have eliminated the impossible, whatever remains, however improbable, must be the truth."
—Sherlock Holmes

Your team hasn't responded to your series of questions even though they usually do so within twenty-four hours. The launch of your new product didn't create a peak in sales even though your focus groups seemed enthusiastic. A potential housemate turned down an offer to live with you even though on paper, it would have been a perfect match.

When you're confronted with competing theories that explain a situation equally well, how do you decide which one to go for? Scholastic philosopher William of Ockham, also spelled as Occam, would give you the following advice: Pick the *simplest* explanation. In other words, don't make more assumptions than you absolutely need, and remove any part of the theory that cannot be observed.

This advice became known as Occam's razor, which can be a helpful addition to your toolbox. Although Occam's razor is 600 years old, it is just as sharp today as it was back then and continues to encourage a skeptical attitude toward unnecessary speculations.

Sharpening Occam's Razor

Time is not always on your side. Some complex decisions deserve to be treated like PhD projects, but unlike in academia, you don't have the opportunity to think through every detail.

Take a moment to think about a recent surprise. What could be three possible explanations for this unforeseen situation? Which explanation has the most assumptions? Which one is the most straightforward? Which one would Occam choose?

Now consider a current project you're working on. What are the predicted results? What do you need to believe for these results to materialize? Is there another, more likely expected outcome? Are there simpler ways to achieve those same results?

Creating Your Own Razor

The Austrian-British philosopher Ludwig Wittgenstein once said, *"If a sign is not necessary, then it is meaningless. That is the meaning of Occam's razor."*

The above is not to say Occam's razor is always the right tool for every situation. You must of course consider the consequences of your decision, especially in the case it turns out to be wrong. At times, you might even be better off with other philosophical razors:

Hitchens's razor: "What can be asserted without evidence can be dismissed without evidence."

Hanlon's razor: "Never attribute to malice that which can be adequately explained by stupidity."

Alder's razor: "What cannot be settled by experiment is not worth debating."

Do you have any razors of your own that help you sufficiently cut through the noise? Which razors help you prevent unnecessary work? Which razor(s) would you like to introduce to your team(s)? Which new one could you create for future generations?

In a complex world that can feel overwhelming at times, keeping things simple can be an elegant way to save yourself and others significant time and mental energy. Just make sure you learn to apply these razors in the right way over time so you don't accidentally cut yourself in the process.

Thoughts, Ideas & More...

Thoughts, Ideas & More...

Hippocrates Can Help You Prevent Unintended Harm

An airline manufacturer wanted to improve the passengers' experience on its planes, so engineers created a new technology that drastically reduced noise in the cabin during flight.

A group of day care centers were tired of parents picking up their kids after hours and, with the help of researchers Uri Gneezy and Aldo Rustichini, experimented with a fine that charged parents if they arrived late to pick up their child.

A celebrity whose private beach house was pictured on an online map filed a legal request to have the photo taken down, hoping to restore the lost privacy.

In each instance, it seemed like the problem was elegantly solved.

However...

The airline manufacturer soon received complaints that the cabin was *too quiet*, resulting in passengers hearing unwanted sounds that were previously drowned out.

Parents who used to pick up their kids on time now also started arriving late: paying the fine alleviated the guilt and, in fact, gave them implicit permission to do so.

The photo of the celebrity's house gained more attention than ever because of the lawsuit, ensuring more people heard about the house than otherwise would have been the case.

These examples demonstrate the difference between "first-order" and "second-order" effects: the immediate consequences of our actions and the (unintended) consequences of these consequences.

Preventing Unintended Harm

Hippocrates of Kos lived around 400 BC and is known as the father of medicine. His legacy still lives on today around the world, from the systematic study of disease to the philosophy and ethics of medical interventions, including the famous Hippocratic Oath for physicians.

The ways of thinking that the Hippocratic school of medicine introduced not only benefited the medical profession but in a broader sense, anyone who wanted to solve a problem in a complex system. An important insight was that *good intentions don't automatically lead to good results* due to many unforeseen consequences of the consequences of one's actions. One's responsibility when attempting to do good is therefore to *"first, do no harm."*

This isn't intended to discourage idealistic people who want to invest their time, creativity, and energy in making a positive difference. This is, however, intended to show that in the end, it's not about the intentions, dreams, or plans on paper. After the consequences of the consequences of the actions have occurred, is the patient better than before? Did we solve the problem? Did the world become a (slightly) better place?

Avoiding Moments of Zugzwang

There is a term in chess known as zugzwang that is defined as a situation "wherein one player is put at a disadvantage because of their obligation to make a move." In other words, the fact that the player is *compelled to move* in this situation means that their position becomes significantly weaker.

When we're confronted with a problem, our natural impulse can be to solve it through immediate action. We might believe, possibly incorrectly, that the situation demands a direct response—that we're *compelled to move*—and that any action in this case is always better than no action.

When we consider second-order effects, however, we might foresee that the unintended consequences of our actions could make the situation even worse than it already is. The harm is often not in the immediate effect but hidden further in the chain of consequences.

Fortunately, life in many ways *doesn't* resemble chess. You might have more options, ranging from not intervening at all to testing various solutions on a small scale in different areas over time. The latter would allow you to better oversee the unintended consequences, get immediate feedback to course correct, develop more effective solutions with each step, and at least prevent large-scale, unintended, and irreversible harm.

Being a Non-Naive Idealist

Think about an important problem you would like to solve right now. Consider the obvious actions that could solve this problem in a clear, drastic, or simple way. If you were to intervene with those actions, what would be the first-order consequences? What would be the second-order consequences? How would you know?

Now assume you took different, more thoughtful actions to solve the problem but somehow still made the situation worse (a so-called *pre-mortem* exercise). You can now work backward to determine what went wrong along the way. With that knowledge, you could make the right and timely decisions to help prevent that outcome from happening.

In the spirit of Hippocrates: as beautiful as our intentions, dreams, and ideals might be, eventually it's the *results* that matter. How could you prevent simplistic solutions from causing unintended harm at scale? How could you make a local problematic situation better through trial and error? When and where will action be better than non-action or the other way around?

Leaving the world better than you found it starts with *at least* not making things worse. With that as your solid foundation, you can freely invest the rest of your inspiration, courage, and idealism in making a positive difference, one consequence (of a consequence) at a time.

Thoughts, Ideas & More...

Thoughts, Ideas & More...

Kant Can Provide You the Courage to Think for Yourself

With today's opportunities to follow the opinions of more people than ever, it's become easier to outsource many aspects of our thinking. From your health to your finances, you only need to find the right expert(s), after which, not much thinking is required on your part.

This sort of cognitive autopilot can also exist in our professional lives. You might work in an organization where answers mainly come from specialists and senior leaders, or there's an established way of doing things that's based on decades of success.

On a day-to-day basis, an environment like this might cultivate a sense of stability, certainty, simplicity, and clarity in an otherwise VUCA world. Underneath the surface, however, there might be unspoken doubts lingering: What if the specialists aren't right? What if the senior leaders are stuck in internal politics? What if the existing processes have become mere rituals, inherited from a glorified past, that don't serve a practical purpose anymore?

In the above instances, German philosopher Immanuel Kant would say, *"Sapere aude"* or *"Dare to know."* Across his dazzling amount of writing—over 1,500 pages published during the Enlightenment—Kant developed his thoughts on a broad range of topics and attempted to answer three fundamental questions:

1. What can I know?
2. What should I do?
3. What may I hope for?

For those in search of ways to think for themselves, these questions can provide an enriching start.

What Can I Know?

Kant believed certain things can be known, while many things are *unknowable*. It's helpful (and humbling) to be able to make a distinction between the two. Thinking this through also gives us the necessary courage to challenge those who claim to know the unknowable.

It's difficult to be skeptical if you think (almost) everything is knowable. It's tempting to react to an expert or authority figure's claim by saying, "This person has decades of experience studying this topic. Who am I to question these statements?" But if you examine what there is to know, you'll be more comfortable borrowing a line mentioned earlier from Socrates: "*Is that really so?*"

Furthermore, a real expert would probably be the first to admit what many great thinkers have written over the centuries: "The more you know, the more you realize you don't know."

With every decision, there are limits to what we *can* know. Analyzing more information to fill in those gaps is not always possible, nor is it ultimately the best use of our time. How will you proceed wisely, then, given all these "known and unknown" unknowns?

What Should I Do?

At any given moment, there are many things in life that you *could* do, but how well do you know what you *should* do? One important area Kant focused on was how we should treat others. Are we going about things the right way? What *should* we do when it comes to those around us?

In the pursuit of our aspirations, there is a risk of considering people as a "resource" or a "means to an end." Kant would argue that people are an *end in themselves* and need to be treated as such. To see things any other way would be an immoral act and a disservice to yourself and others.

How often do you make a clear distinction between "means" and "ends"? How do you prevent mixing these up in your decision making, at work and otherwise? How *should* you treat friends, family, neighbors, colleagues, strangers, the rest of nature, or yourself? And why?

What May I Hope For?

As discussed earlier, there are certain things in life we can never know. But that doesn't mean we can't hope for them to be true.

What are your hopes, dreams, and wishes for yourself for the future? What about your community and the organization where you work? What are your hopes about life in general? In case you have forgotten about them, Kant would encourage you to practice developing and pursuing your ideals. Especially in the face of a continuous stream of disappointments, idealism can be difficult to maintain, but as the expression goes, "If not now, then when?" If you would dare to speak it, what would you dare to hope for this year?

Finding Your Own Answers

Sticking with the status quo or following expert advice can feel comfortable in the short term or, for some, even in the long term. But looking back from the future, is that how you would have wanted to live your life? What if others turn out to be wrong? What if they turn out to be right? Independent of what others might say, why not also use your own wondrous faculty of reason and thinking to the best of your abilities?

What can I know? What should I do? What may I hope for?

Kant had his own answers, but he probably wouldn't want you to blindly follow them. He'd want you to think deeply, to revise, add, or remove things based on your own judgment, and to arrive at your own conclusions.

At least that's what we *can* and *should* hope for.

Thoughts, Ideas & More...

Thoughts, Ideas & More...

Hipparchia Can Show You the Right Direction Based on Your Values

There are moments in life where you encounter a *clear* answer to a *complex* problem: your financial calculations determine that you shouldn't invest in a business idea, the law requires specific clauses you need to include in a new contract, or you've experienced a certain situation so often before that the course ahead is quite evident.

However, sometimes the answer isn't obvious: there is an urgent crisis where you can't fully research all the options, your customer asks for a new service that requires a significant investment from your side, you're considering whether to move to a new place and can't easily weigh certain choices, or you need to find the best way to spend an unexpected free moment.

In these ambiguous situations, even when you do get the chance to ask those you trust for advice, recommendations can be all over the board. You want to ensure you make the best decision (or at least one that you won't regret), but you're not sure which direction to go.

During these moments, the decisions of Hipparchia, a Cynic philosopher from around 300 BC, can serve as a guiding example. Many of her writings and ideas were unfortunately lost with the passage of time, but what endures is her example of living according to her values.

When her family tried to convince her otherwise, she chose *love* and married the philosopher Crates. When others around her were consumed with making money, she chose to live *unattached to material things*. In the face of certain expectations of her role in a household, she fought for *equality*. When others sought pleasure, she sought *wisdom* instead.

When we want to make sound choices, our values can certainly help us in *any* situation, but in ambiguous moments like the ones mentioned above, their importance is *especially* clear. Like a compass in a disorienting storm, our values can point us in the right direction and give us the courage to pull through.

But this immediately raises an important question: *How well do you know your values?* How aware of them are you, how do they relate to each other, and how often do you put them into practice?

What Are Your Values?

Values are deeply held beliefs that can guide your attitude and actions. They help you distinguish between what is right or wrong, what is import-ant or a distraction, what is desirable or unaccept-able. Values can measure whether your life is on the right path and whether you're making the right trade-offs. They can provide a sense of fulfillment when you take actions aligned with them or make you feel pain when they are breached.

Some values might have always existed in you, while others are shaped, perhaps by your upbring-ing, your work environment, or your community. As interesting as it might be to further discover *where* they came from, for now, we'll start with *what* they are for you today.

Some examples of values include Adventure, Originality, Loyalty, Freedom, Courage, Ambi-tion, Honesty, Playfulness, Creativity, Growth,

Mastery, and Love. In addition, you can find a broader selection on the page titled "With Gratitude," where you're free to add as many as you like.

Take a moment to explore the full list and see if you can answer for yourself the following:

- Do any values resonate more with you than others?

- As much as all of them can be important to others, which ones are important to *you*?

- Which ones do you find beautiful, helpful, and inspirational or, in other words, *valuable*?

- Are there any values that you wish to have as an integral part of your life?

- Do any values give you sufficient meaning by

themselves, or do they need to be combined with others?

- Could you select, or even rank, a top five?

Living Your Values in the Real World

Once you have a better view of which values resonate most with you, you can start asking yourself to what extent you feel you take actions in life *consistent* with your values. Not only when things are obvious and easy but especially when moments are difficult and ambiguous or when there is tension *between* your values. When you face tough decisions, are you willing to pay a price to live according to your values like Hipparchia? If not, can you still say you *truly* hold those values? Over time, through testing your values in the real world, you can gain a clearer view of which ones mean the most to you.

And of course, the better you understand yourself, the better you'll understand those around you. Are there shared values within your family or team? How well do you know the values of the five people you work most with? Are there values that strengthen each other or (at least on the surface) complement or even contradict each other? What would be a wise way to take this into consideration when making decisions?

Outcomes may feel out of your control at times, at work and beyond. However, if you know and live your values, at least *the path forward* and *the person you become* is congruent with what you find most important in life. In other words, you will have the freedom to make each difficult step worthwhile in and of itself, especially if your values are clear.

Thoughts, Ideas & More...

Thoughts, Ideas & More...

Bringing It All Together

Over two millennia ago, Aristotle wrote that "it is the mark of an educated mind to be able to entertain a thought without accepting it." It can be intellectually satisfying to enrich your personal worldview, but on a much more practical level, developing a rich life philosophy and different ways of thinking can also help you make better decisions in a world that feels increasingly volatile, unpredictable, complex, and ambiguous.

Exposing yourself to different philosophies over time allows you to practice various tools and approaches to solve difficult problems that will inevitably come your way. These tools and approaches are not about what you *should* do but about what you *could* do. As you better understand the latter, you can better decide what you *want* to do.

As a way to practice, let's explore three contexts most likely familiar to you—new opportunities, obstacles, and surprises—and see how different thinkers throughout history might have approached the situation.

Handling a New Opportunity

At some point in your career, you might encounter an exciting opportunity such as starting a new company or launching a new product. We can imagine Socrates and Nietzsche debating how they would advise you to handle this decision. Socrates was known for asking, "*Is that really so?*" When applied correctly, this skeptical approach can help you avoid (irreversible) mistakes.

Using this approach, you can ask yourself critically, "Is this *really* an opportunity, or does it only *appear* to be one?" You'd also want to know what could go wrong and perhaps develop a plan to prevent undesirable things from happening. Even if the chance of failure is small, what price would you have to pay if failure *does* somehow materialize?

On the other side is Nietzsche and his thought experiment on eternal recurrence. If this exact moment were to repeat itself forever into eternity, would you be happy to relive it an infinite number of times?

By putting infinite weight on your decision this way, you can get clarity on one important question: *What do you want?* If you've always wanted to launch a new company or product, would it matter if it's successful or not?

Could you live with the decision *not to go after* what you want if that decision echoed into eternity? How would you advise yourself if you could do so from the distant future?

Overcoming an Obstacle

You're working toward an important goal and reach an unexpected obstacle right in front of you. As you decide how to handle this unforeseen situation, let's consider the philosophies of Aristotle and Bruce Lee.

Aristotle saw challenging situations as opportunities to develop virtues: character traits that are considered to be positive. As you think about the person you'd like to become, consider what virtues you would need to develop in order to build your character. Are you using life's challenges as opportunities to develop those virtues?

It is only when we are *tempted to give up* that we can practice *diligence*, only when we *worry about the consequences* that we can practice *honesty*, and only when we *face real fear* that we can practice *courage*. The same logic applies to practicing humility, compassion, patience, generosity, kindness, or any other virtue that is meaningful to you.

However, if you look at it from the philosophy of "be water" as Bruce Lee would famously say, these obstacles were maybe not meant to be overcome through blood, sweat, and tears but with as little friction as possible. Water doesn't get jammed up in a river when confronted with a rock. Instead, it flows around obstacles and continues downstream. It doesn't underreact, overreact, or stop. It flows to the best of its ability, exactly as it needs, depending on the situation. Maybe wisdom in this situation means not fighting *through the obstacle* but finding an *elegant way around it*.

Dealing with Surprises

Surprises can catch you off guard. Whether good or bad, it can take time to wrap your mind around what's happening and determine what to do. Thales and Democritus offer two different ways of dealing with surprises.

Thales was adept at recognizing patterns. He might tell you to stop and consider if what is happening has happened before, and if so, what followed? When you are good at noticing short- and long-term patterns on a large and local scale, you will be less surprised and better prepared for anything that comes your way.

On the other hand, Democritus knew our tendency to view the world through a lens of too much theory instead of clearly observing our present reality as it unfolds from the eternal here and now. Therefore, his primary concern wasn't necessarily recognizing patterns over time but mainly that which was right in front of us. Don't miss the fire because "each year around this time, the weather gets a bit warmer over here." Start with your five senses: hear, see, taste, touch, and smell what is going on around you.

Now, How about You?

When one wants to learn how to cook new and nourishing dishes, one can start with classic recipes that have been tried, tested, and improved by innumerable ancestors in the past. Similarly, a helpful step to further develop and enrich your own philosophy is to study tools from innumerable thinkers who have wondered about life before you.

Enjoy. And who knows? One day, you may do your part by passing on wisdom to a new generation. In your own unique way, you will help people make better decisions and add to what others have generously, courageously, and kindly done for us so far.

Thoughts, Ideas & More...

Thoughts, Ideas & More...

What Is Wisdom?

In your own words, if no one would ever know your answer.

What Is Wisdom?

What Is Wisdom?

With Gratitude

This book couldn't have been created without the help of so many eternal values that have been passed on from generation to generation since ancient times, like adding complementary figures to a colorful mosaic.

It was a delight to see these values come to life, in the words of Aristotle, *at the right time, to the right degree, for the right purpose, and in the right way*, through the actions of family, friends, neighbors, colleagues, classmates, teachers, strangers, and countless other beautiful souls:

Love, Acceptance, Beauty, Competence, Discipline, Loyalty, Support, Accomplishment, Concentration, Discovery, Growth, Mastery, Rigor, Surprise, Humor, Confidence, Drive, Teamwork, Adaptability, Happiness, Maturity, Satisfaction, Connection, Effectiveness, Vitality, Harmony, Motivation, Security, Adventure, Consciousness, Efficiency, Health, Openness, Self-Reliance, Timeliness, Ambition, Consistency, Resourcefulness, Empathy, Honesty, Optimism, Sensitivity, Amusement, Tradition, Contentment, Endurance, Restraint, Success, Honor, Order, Serenity, Logic, Assertiveness, Contribution, Energy, Humility, Spontaneity, Organization, Service, Control, Peace, Imagination, Originality, Sharing, Understanding, Delight, Balance, Excellence, Conviction, Enthusiasm, Independence, Passion, Dignity, Significance, Uniqueness, Boldness, Awe, Cooperation, Excellence, Integrity, Altruism, Hope, Silence, Unity, Tolerance, Bravery, Experience, Truthfulness, Persistence, Simplicity, Courtesy, Exploration, Intensity, Playfulness, Sincerity, Victory, Creativity,

Fairness, Joy, Certainty, Credibility, Justice, Professionalism, Solitude, Reverence, Vision, Challenge, Curiosity, Focus, Kindness, Charity, Decisiveness, Authenticity, Reason, Wealth, Dependability, Freedom, Learning, Recognition, Stability, Comfort, Determination, Fun, Liberty, Recreation, Strength, Commitment, Devotion, Generosity, Trust, Respect, Structure, Courage, Compassion, Awareness, and Wonder.

About the Author

Kayvan Kian is an entrepreneur, teacher, and senior advisor to McKinsey & Company in Amsterdam, whose work has helped thousands of leaders and teams thrive during difficult times.

As the founder of the Young Leaders Forum, Kayvan has given guest lectures at Harvard Business School, HEC, Sciences Po, and more. His first book, *What Is Water?: How Young Leaders Can Thrive in an Uncertain World*, became an instant bestseller. He holds an MBA from INSEAD in France and a degree in both Economics and Law from the Erasmus University in the Netherlands.

www.kayvankian.com

More by Kayvan Kian

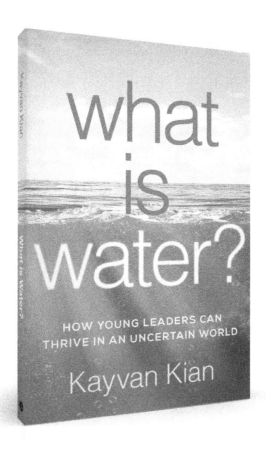

what
is
water?

HOW YOUNG LEADERS CAN
THRIVE IN AN UNCERTAIN WORLD

Kayvan Kian

Look!

Did you see it?

CPSIA information can be obtained
at www.ICGtesting.com
Printed in the USA
BVHW030349140422
634269BV00005B/7

9 781544 524368